WE

A R E   T H E

MANY

A PICTURE BOOK
OF AMERICAN INDIANS

BY DOREEN RAPPAPORT

ILLUSTRATED BY CORNELIUS VAN WRIGHT

AND YING-HWA HU

HARPERCOLLINSPUBLISHERS

AUTHOR'S NOTE

The first inhabitants of the Americas were people now called Indians. For thousands of years before Europeans arrived, they lived in what is now the United States. There were hundreds of groups of Indian people. In 1492 more than five hundred languages were spoken. Indian children learned their people's history from their elders. They listened to their grandmothers and grandfathers tell stories about what happened in the past and explain religious practices and other traditions. When they grew up, they passed on the stories and traditions to their children. And so knowledge went from generation to generation.

Each story in this book re-creates one moment in a person's life. It opens in 1621, when Tisquantum taught the Pilgrims to find and plant food. It ends 370 years later with Sherman Alexie writing a poem. The people I wrote about did many different things. Osceola was a warrior. Lone Dog was a historian. Lyda Conley was a lawyer. Jim Thorpe was one of the greatest athletes who ever lived. It was hard choosing only sixteen people: There are thousands more whose achievements are important to American history. Think of this book as the start of your journey to learning about American Indians.

You will see that some people have two names. The first name is their Indian name. Sometimes people have difficulty reproducing words in a foreign language. European settlers wrote down what they thought they heard. Most Americans know Tisquantum as Squanto. "Squanto" is probably what the Pilgrims thought they heard, but some American Indians believe neither name was his real name. As Americans forced Indians to adopt their way of life, Indians were given new names. Some Indians kept using their Indian names. Native speakers and linguists helped me translate the Indian names and words and provided the pronunciations on page 31.

CONTENTS

TISQUANTUM

SQUANTO CA. 1589-1622

PATUXET

A disease brought by white explorers had wiped out Tisquantum's people. Now people from England were living where their village used to be, in what we call Plymouth, Massachusetts. This past winter hunger and cold had killed half the Pilgrims. More would die if they did not learn how to survive in this new land. Tisquantum knew he must help them.

He showed the Pilgrims how to weave tall, thick grass into fishing nets. They lowered the nets into a rushing stream. Soon the nets were heavy with trout and small bass and alewives. Tisquantum put the trout and bass aside for eating. He took the alewives to the newly plowed fields. Loosen the soil and build small hills, he instructed. From a small deerskin pouch, he took out the precious gift of corn seed. He planted four seeds in each hill. Good farmers plant extra seeds to guard against beetles and crows and cutworms, he explained. He buried three alewives in each hill. The nitrogen in the fish helped enrich the soil for growing corn.

In early December 1622, the Pilgrims invited Tisquantum and other Wampanoag Indians to a harvest feast to thank them for their help. Today Thanksgiving is a national holiday celebrated on the fourth Thursday in November.

KOÑWATSI'TSIÉÑNI

MOLLY BRANT CA. 1736–1796
MOHAWK

Molly barred the door. She stretched out her legs and closed her eyes. How quiet it was. She welcomed the silence. *Bang! Bang!* Who was pounding at the door? Was it British soldiers needing help? Molly sided with the English in their war against the American colonists. She believed the British would stop the Americans from taking more land from her people.

Bang! Bang! Or was it patriots come to arrest her? Molly's English husband had been in charge of Indian relations in the northern colonies. He had died recently. His relatives warned Molly that she was in danger now and should move back to her village, Canajoharie, on the Mohawk River, in what we today call New York State.

Her knees trembled as she walked toward the door. She opened it slowly. Two men were leaning on the doorjamb. Their red uniforms meant they were British soldiers. She hurried them inside. She warmed up supper and made a place for them to sleep. You can stay here for a while, she assured them.

During the Revolutionary War, Molly Brant helped British soldiers and Americans who stayed loyal to England. When the Americans won the war, she fled to Canada. The British rewarded her by giving her money to live on for the rest of her life.

SHUNKA-ISHNALA

LONE DOG CA. 1780–1871
YANKTONAI DAKOTA

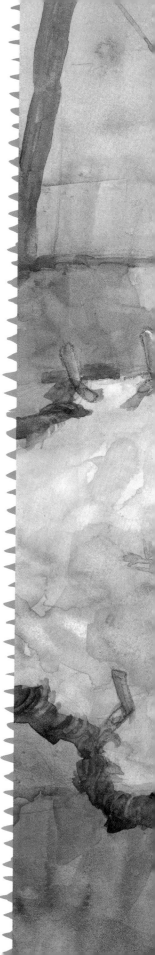

Lone Dog looked at the pictures painted on the buffalo skin. Each one told a different story. The figure with red dots stood for the year many of his people died from measles, the disease brought by white settlers. There were happy stories, too. There was the year the men captured many wild horses. And the year when the buffalo were so numerous they grazed near the tepees.

When Lone Dog was little, he learned his people's history by listening to the tribal historian. Now he was the historian. Every year he met with the elders to choose one important event to paint. This year's picture would show the brilliant ball of fire that had streaked across the sky.

He picked up his brush whittled from wood. The tip was made of antelope hair. He dipped it into water, then into red paint made from clay. He painted a burst of red for the exploding meteor. A black line showed its fall to earth.

Lone Dog's calendar is called a winter count because his people counted their years in winters. On cold nights, in the winter camp in what is now Standing Rock, North Dakota, the snow whipped about Lone Dog's teepee. He sat by the fire and told the children the stories behind the pictures. He passed on his people's history as it had been passed on to him.

SACAJAWEA CA. 1788-1812
SHOSHONE

One hour. Two hours. Sacajawea trudged along the riverbank with her baby on her back. The August air was hot and sticky. Not a hint of a breeze. Three hours. Four hours. Mosquitoes nipped at her neck and arms. Needle grass pricked her feet.

Finally she saw a grassy plain dotted with sunflowers and lamb's-quarter. Beyond the plain were mountains. She knew this place. She and her mother had gathered wild artichokes here. Five years ago a raiding party of Hidatsa Indians had taken her from her family here. She had not seen them since.

Now the leaders of this expedition were looking for her people. They needed horses and a guide. The white men did not know this part of the country. But Sacajawea did. You are close to my people's camp, she assured them. She pointed to a hill she called Beaver's Head.

Five days later they arrived at the Shoshone camp in the state now called Idaho. Sacajawea was reunited with her brother, Cameahwait, who was now a chief. He sold horses to William Clark and Meriwether Lewis. He gave them a guide to lead them west through the winding creeks and ravines and over the mountains.

Sacajawea was the only woman on the Lewis and Clark expedition westward to find a path to the Pacific Ocean. At different times she acted as guide, food gatherer, and interpreter.

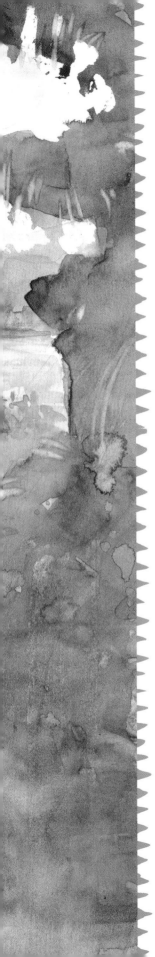

ASIYAHOLA OSCEOLA 1804-1838
SEMINOLE

Down! Osceola signaled his warriors. They hid in the underbrush on the south bank of the Withlacoochee River in Florida. More than four hundred American soldiers were on the other side of the river. They had come to force the Seminoles off their land again. Osceola was determined this would not happen.

Back and forth. Back and forth. Osceola watched the Americans paddle across the river. Now sixty Americans were on his side. They laid their guns on the bank and rested. *Now!* Osceola signaled his warriors. The air exploded with rifle shot. The Americans raced in circles, trying to escape the bullets from the invisible enemy.

An American soldier spotted Osceola. He was wearing a blue Army jacket, a trophy of a past victory. The soldier carefully aimed his rifle. *Now!* Osceola fell backward. His rifle fell to the ground. He clutched his shoulder. It felt like it was burning. But he did not let that stop him. He picked up his gun and fired. Osceola's warriors won this battle in the Second Seminole War.

For two years his army fought to keep their land in Florida. In 1837, sick from malaria, he called a truce. The Americans agreed, then tricked him. They imprisoned him and some of his followers. He died three months later. Other Seminoles took up the fight. By 1843 most had been captured and forced to leave their homes and move to Indian territory, now called Oklahoma.

SUSAN LA FLESCHE PICOTTE 1865–1915
OMAHA

The wind on the Nebraska plain howled and bit into Susan's face. She draped her shawl over her head and around her neck. Thick snowflakes swirled in front of her. It was hard to see the roads on the reservation. Perhaps it had not been wise to come out in such a snowstorm. But she had to see if the child with pneumonia was better.

The turn to the cabin was somewhere ahead. But where? Off to the right, gray smoke streaked the sky. Was the smoke coming from the cabin where the child lived? When the reservation had been created, the Omahas had been forced to leave their earth lodges and move into log cabins. She turned her horse toward the gray cloud. When she reached the cabin, she tied her horse to a post. She took her medical bag and trudged through the deep snow. By the time she reached the cabin door, her feet were soaked. She knocked gently and waited to be invited in.

Susan La Flesche Picotte was the daughter of Iron Eyes, a chief of the Omaha Nation. In 1889 she graduated from the Women's Medical College of Pennsylvania. She returned to the reservation. Susan traveled by horseback through dust storms and snowstorms to care for her people. She was the only doctor for the thirteen hundred Omahas. Her people honored her by naming the hospital she established after her.

HELENA CONLEY 1867–1958;
IDA CONLEY CA. 1862–1948;
LYDA CONLEY 1869–1946
WYANDOT

Helena looked up from her book. Her eyes met her sister Ida's. She had heard the noise, too. Was it leaves rustling or footsteps? Had someone climbed over the padlocked gates of the cemetery? Perhaps they had not believed the sign, TRESPASS AT YOUR PERIL. Ida picked up the shotgun. The two sisters left the caretaker's shack where they lived and went looking for intruders among their ancestors' graves.

Lyda continued writing. She was a lawyer. Lyda would soon plead her people's case before the U.S. Supreme Court. She would show the judges proof that the Wyandots had bought this land sixty-five years ago. She would explain that her family and important chiefs were buried here. No one had the right to remove their bones from this sacred land. The Wyandots would never dig up the graves of George Washington or any other Americans.

The Court ruled against the Wyandots. But the sisters kept fighting to save the cemetery in Kansas City, Kansas. For seven years they guarded it by living there. They gave speeches. Congressman Charles Curtis, who was Kaw and Osage, joined their fight. Finally, in 1913, Congress declared that the land belonged to the Wyandots. The cemetery is now on the National Registry of Historic Places. The Conley sisters are buried there.

WATHA HUCK JIM THORPE 1887–1953
SAUK AND FOX

Jim leaned forward and listened for the starting gun. It was the last race in the pentathlon. If he won this 1,500-meter race, he would win an Olympic gold medal.

Bang! Two men darted out and took the lead. Jim was way behind them. One thousand meters to go. He pumped his arms and picked up the pace. He passed one runner. Then another. Faster, faster. Three hundred meters left. His legs flew off the ground as he crossed the finish line. The crowd roared.

Jim Thorpe won two gold medals at the 1912 Olympic Games in Stockholm, Sweden. One was for the pentathlon, a five-event track-and-field sport. The other was for the ten-event decathlon.

A month later it was discovered that Jim had accepted a few dollars when playing semiprofessional baseball. In those days athletes who competed in the Olympics were not allowed to play sports for money. The Olympic Committee took back Jim's medals. His name was erased from the record books. People all over the world protested: Other athletes had done the same thing, but they had not been punished. Why had this happened to one of the world's greatest athletes?

Sixty-one years later, in 1973, the Olympic Committee apologized to Jim's family and returned his medals to them. Today the medals can be seen under his portrait in the state capitol in Oklahoma City.

MARÍA MARTÍNEZ 1887–1980;
JULIÁN MARTÍNEZ 1897–1943
SAN ILDEFONSO PUEBLO

María mixed clay and ash with water. She kneaded it, as if making bread. Pinch, press. Pinch, press. On an old plate she formed the base of an *olla,* a water jar. Between her palms she rolled a long even rope. With one hand she turned the plate. With the other she wound the clay rope around the base. She wound one coil on top of another until the walls were tall.

She smoothed the walls with a piece of gourd and let the *olla* dry in the sun. Then she smoothed it again with special stones. She applied a thin mixture of clay and water and stone-polished it again.

Julián picked up his paintbrush. The tip was made from fibers of yucca plants. He dipped it into black paint that he had made from clay and boiled wild spinach. With careful strokes he painted feathers on the *olla.* Then he baked it in a fire pit. It came out all shiny, except where he had painted the feathers. María and Julián's pottery looked different from any pottery made then.

María taught other potters in the San Ildefonso Pueblo in New Mexico how to make this "black-on-black" pottery. Her son and grandson and great-granddaughter and great-great-grandson are among the many who carried on this tradition she had rediscovered from thousands of years ago.

WILLIAM McCABE 1915-1976
NAVAJO

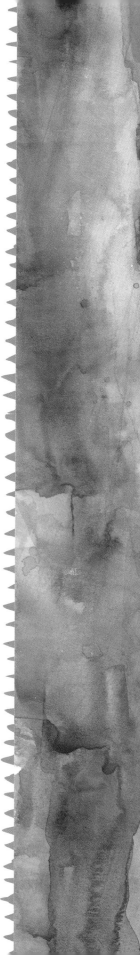

William held his eighty-pound radio over his head and crawled along the sand. When he reached seven-foot-tall grass, he stood and hacked his way through the sharp blades. Poisonous snakes darted underfoot. From behind coconut trees, Japanese soldiers fired machine guns at him and the other marines. William tried not to look at the fallen bodies all around him.

On the other side of the jungle, he and his partner dug a foxhole. His partner cranked up the power of their radio. Then William sent a coded message in Navajo to headquarters, asking for more troops. Japanese codebreakers heard him speaking on their radios. They could not understand one word.

William McCabe was one of 420 Navajo code talkers. During World War II, the code talkers sent thousands of secret messages during battles in the Pacific Islands. Their messages helped win the war. William McCabe helped create the code. Code words came from familiar things in Navajo life. Airplanes were named after birds. Dive bombers were *gini*, or hawks. Ships were named after fish. A submarine was *baash-lo*, or iron fish. This brilliant code was never broken by the enemy.

Twenty-nine code talkers received the Congressional Gold Medal. The remaining code talkers and their survivors received the Congressional Silver Medal in 2001.

MARIA TALLCHIEF 1925-
OSAGE

Up went the curtain on the second act of *The Nutcracker* ballet. It was Christmas Eve. The handsome Nutcracker Prince had taken a girl named Clara on a magical journey to the Kingdom of Sweets. On pointed toe the Sugar Plum Fairy swept onto the stage like a gentle breeze. Maria Tallchief was a vision in pink, with sequins on her skirt and tiara. She sat Clara and the Prince on a candy throne and gave them sweets. Then she danced.

Up on her pink toe shoes, she stretched her arms like birds' wings ready to fly. She bent forward and lifted her left leg. Her chest swept down toward the floor. She straightened up again. She curved her arms and raised them over her head. Up, up she lifted her left leg again. A man came forward and twirled her. She was a shimmering swirl of pink. The tempo slowed. Her arms fluttered down to her sides. The tempo quickened. She stretched her arms out and spun across the stage, a whirl of grace and beauty.

Maria Tallchief grew up on a reservation in Fairfax, Oklahoma. On a summer vacation in Colorado when she was three, she took her first ballet lesson. When she returned home, she took piano lessons. She was extremely talented in both music and dance, but dance won her heart. As a famous ballerina, she danced all over the world and captured the hearts of kings and queens and children. One of her most beloved roles was the Sugar Plum Fairy.

WILMA MANKILLER 1949-

CHEROKEE

Wilma pushed her shovel into the earth. She scooped up dirt and threw it behind her. Then into the earth again went her shovel. The day was cool, but sweat ringed her neck and soaked her shirt. The shovel was heavier with each thrust. Her arms ached.

She looked down the row of bent backs pushing shovels into the earth. Wilma was part of a team. Her team had to lay two miles of a twenty-six-mile water pipeline. When it was installed, there would be no more hauling water in plastic milk jugs from the school well. No more worrying about dry summers. Soon every one of the one hundred and five families in Bell, Oklahoma, would have enough water. Wilma picked up her shovel and began digging again.

Wilma Mankiller was the first woman chief of the Cherokee Nation of Oklahoma. She believes that people should do things for one another and for their communities. When the pipeline was finished, she thought up another project. Her people built twenty-five new houses for themselves and rebuilt twenty old ones. After the houses were built, she set up a health clinic. After that, a vocational training center. In her thirteen years of leadership, she completed many projects to make her people more self-reliant.

SHERMAN ALEXIE 1966-
SPOKANE-COEUR D'ALENE

Sherman Alexie looked at the photograph taken at Monument Valley High School on the Navajo reservation in Kayenta, Arizona. Here Navajo children learned their people's history and language, along with math and science and reading and writing. He wrote a poem about the school's young athletes.

> the football field rises
> to meet the mesa. Indian boys
> gallop across the grass, against
>
> the beginning of their body.
>
> . . . Before the game is over,
> The eighth-grade girls' track team
>
> comes running, circling the field
> their thin and brown legs echoing
> wild horses, wild horses, wild horses.

Sherman Alexie was born on the Spokane Indian Reservation in Wellpinit, Washington. He writes poems, novels, stories, and screenplays. His first film, *Smoke Signals,* was set on the reservation. The hero is a smart boy named Thomas Builds-The-Fire. Sherman Alexie loves the movies, because "they continue the oral tradition, the way we all sit around the fire and listen to stories."

ABOUT THIS BOOK

WHEN WRITING THIS BOOK, I read it to children in different schools. The questions that popped up the most were "Are these stories true? How do you know what happened three and four hundred years ago?" To write these vignettes, I read newspaper articles, diaries, journals, interviews, first-person accounts, and books by historians. I checked the sources against one another to write the truest account possible.

I found first-person accounts by William McCabe and Wilma Mankiller. William Bradford, governor of Plymouth, wrote about Tisquantum's help. To write about Molly Brant, I read articles by historians and imagined a scene. In an old book at the New York Public Library I found Lone Dog's winter count and explanations of the symbols and how he made the drawings. Sacajawea's actions were described in *The Journals of Lewis and Clark*. Military historians have re-created Osceola's battle. Reading about Nebraska snowstorms helped me describe Dr. Picotte's journey. Newspapers detailed the Conley sisters' struggle. Lyda Conley mentioned George Washington in her Supreme Court brief. Sportswriters described Jim Thorpe's race. Books about and photographs of María and Julían Martínez showed them making pottery. I watched a film of Maria Tallchief in *The Nutcracker*. I had a wonderful time reading Sherman Alexie's poems, searching for the one in this book.

I am grateful to Christy Cox; Arlene Hirschfelder; the Wyandotte County Historical Society and Museum, Bonner Springs, Kansas; Sam and Patsy Billison of the Navajo Code Talkers Association; and to Susan Dingle of the North Dakota Historical Society for answering my many questions. I thank the Billisons, Joseph Bruchac, Victor Golla, John Koontz, Wayland Large, Carl Masthay, Gunther Michelson, and Grace Thorpe for helping me with the pronunciation guide.

—*Doreen Rappaport*

ILLUSTRATING *We Are the Many* has been a tremendous opportunity and challenge. We have had a chance to examine the history and lives of the sixteen individuals in this book. Doreen Rappaport shared many of her resources. It was also beneficial that Ying-Hwa had taught a history class and was familiar with some of the historical figures. It was challenging to imagine what people looked like before the camera was invented. What did they wear? What was their environment like? We searched library files, books, and Internet sites for clues. We relied on portraits etched and painted centuries ago. We cross-referenced tribes and neighboring tribes and visited the Smithsonian Museum of the American Indian. Even with all our research, we still had to make some educated guesses and use artistic license at times. Ultimately we believe we have captured and portrayed the essence of each moment in time.

—*Cornelius Van Wright* and *Ying-Hwa Hu*

PRONUNCIATION GUIDE

Asiyahola (AH-see-yah-HO-low) combines two words: *asi,* which means "black tea-like ceremonial drink," and *yahola,* which means "ceremonial cry."

Baash-lo (BAYSH-low) means "iron fish."

Cameahwait (Gah-ME-ah-wait) means "I'll stay here."

Gini (GHI-ni) means "hawk."

Koñwatsi'tsiéñni (Goong-wah-gee'-jah-YAW-nee) means "someone lends her a flower."

Sacajawea: The Shoshone name for Sacajawea (sah-kah-jah-WAY-uh) means "boat puller." The Hidatsa name for Sacagawea (sah-kah-gah-WAY-uh) means "boat woman."

Shunka-Ishnala (SHOONG-kah-ee-SHNAH-lah or SHOONG-kah-eesh-NAH-lah) means "lone dog."

Tisquantum (Tis-SQUAHN-tum) means "angry god."

Watha Huck (WAH-thah Huck) means "bright path."

RESEARCH SOURCES

*Alexie, Sherman. "At Navajo Monument Valley Tribal School," *The Business of Fancydancing,* Brooklyn, N.Y.: Hanging Loose Press, 1992.

Ambrose, Stephen. *Undaunted Courage.* New York: Simon & Schuster, 1996.

Bixler, Margaret T. *Winds of Freedom: The Story of the Navajo Code Talkers of World War II.* Darien, Conn.: Two Bytes Publishing, 1992.

DeVoto, Bernard, ed. *The Journals of Lewis and Clark.* Boston: Houghton Mifflin, 1963.

Hartley, William and Ellen. *Osceola, the Unconquered Indian.* New York: Hawthorn Books, 1973.

Hirschfelder, Arlene, and *Martha Kreipe de Montaño. *The Native American Almanac.* New York: Prentice Hall General Reference, 1993.

Hoxie, Frederick, ed. *Encyclopedia of North American Indians.* Boston: Houghton Mifflin, 1996.

Mahon, John K. *History of the Second Seminole War, 1835–1862.* Gainesville: University of Florida Press, 1967.

Mallery, Garrick. *Picture Writing of the American Indians.* Washington, D.C.: Smithsonian Ethnology Bureau Annual Report, 1893.

*Mankiller, Wilma Pearl. *Mankiller: A Chief and Her People.* New York: St. Martin's Press, 1999.

Marine Corps Historical Center, Washington, D.C., taped interview with William McCabe.

Marriott, Alice. *Maria: The Potter of San Ildefonso.* Norman: University of Oklahoma Press, 1948.

BOOKS FOR YOUNG READERS

Adler, David A. *A Picture Book of Sacagawea.* New York: Holiday House, 2000.

*Begay, Shonto. *Navajo: Voices and Visions Across the Mesa.* New York: Scholastic, 1995.

*Bruchac, Joseph. *Squanto's Journey: The Story of the First Thanksgiving.* Illustrated by Greg Shed. New York: Harcourt Children's Books, 2000.

———. *Sacajawea: The Story of Bird Woman and the Lewis and Clark Expedition.* New York: Harcourt Children's Books, 2000.

Coffey, Wayne. *Jim Thorpe: Athlete of the Century (Olympic Gold).* Woodbridge, Conn.: Blackbirch Press, 1994.

*Crow, Alan. *The Crying Christmas Tree.* Illustrated by David Beyer. Winnipeg, Can.: Pemmican, 1989.

Hirschfelder, Arlene B., and *Beverly. R. Singer, eds. *Rising Voices: Writings of Young Native Americans.* New York: Charles Scribner's Sons, 1992.

Hunter, Sara H. *The Unbreakable Code.* Illustrated by Julia Miner. Flagstaff, Ariz.: Northland, 1996.

*Smith, Cynthia Leitich. *Jingle Dancer.* Illustrated by Cornelius Van Wright and Ying-Hwa Hu. New York: Morrow Junior Books, 2000.

*Sneve, Virginia Driving Hawk. *The Sioux: A First Americans Book.* Illustrated by Ronald Himler. New York: Holiday House, 1995.

*Tallchief, Maria, and Rosemary Wells. *Maria Tallchief: America's Prima Ballerina.* Illustrated by Gary Kelley. New York: Dial Books, 2000.

WEBSITES

www.tc.bostonkids.org (Boston Children's Museum)

www.history.navy.mil/faqs/faq61-4.htm (includes the Navajo Code)

*www.cynthialeitichsmith.com

*www.cradleboard.org

*www.fallsapart.com (Sherman Alexie)

*by Native Americans

For Arlene Hirschfelder,
with deep appreciation for her overwhelming generosity
in sharing her knowledge
—D.R.

To Rosemary, for her encouragement and patience in
allowing us to discover this book's voice
—C.V.W. and Y.-H.H.

We gratefully acknowledge permission to reprint the poem on
page 28: reprinted from *The Business of Fancydancing,* © 1992 by Sherman Alexie,
by permission of Hanging Loose Press.

We thank Ingrid Putesoy for permission to use the title of her poem "We Are The Many"
as the title of this book. The poem was originally published in *The Eye of a White Dove* in
1985. It was written when she was a student at the Havasupai Elementary School.

We Are the Many
Text copyright © 2002 by Doreen Rappaport
Illustrations copyright © 2002 by Cornelius Van Wright and Ying-Hwa Hu
Printed in Singapore. All rights reserved.
www.harperchildrens.com

Library of Congress Cataloging-in-Publication Data
Rappaport, Doreen.
We are the many : a picture book of American Indians / by Doreen Rappaport ;
illustrated by Cornelius Van Wright and Ying-Hwa Hu.
p.   cm.
Summary: A collection of short, illustrated biographies of sixteen influential Native Americans,
from Tisquantum, who helped the Pilgrims survive the winter of 1622, to Sherman Alexie, a
contemporary poet, novelist, and screenwriter.
ISBN 0-688-16559-1 — ISBN 0-06-001139-4 (library binding)
1. Indians of North America—Biography—Juvenile literature.   2. Indians of North America—
History—Juvenile literature.   [1. Indians of North America—Biography.   2. Indians of North
America—History.]   I. Van Wright, Cornelius, ill.   II. Hu, Ying-Hwa, ill.   III. Title.
E89 .R35 2002   970.004'97'00922—dc21   2001039820

Design by Stephanie Bart-Horvath
1 2 3 4 5 6 7 8 9 10
❖
First Edition